...ixed-up pleased queasy ridiculous bashful hopeful
energetic different zonked rambunctious silly quiet overwhelmed
negative sleepy glad insecure disappointed selfish timid impatient joyful upset
sensitive vicious beautiful frustrated knowing irritable vibrant worried moody
generous exhilarated active obnoxious blue calm afraid hyperactive
wild sad vulnerable uneasy bored scared curious pretty nasty lonely doubtful
terrific exhausted excited zealous embarrassed frightened brave giggly
awful weird terrible quarrelsome crazy stubborn happy zany disgusted
intimidated greedy lucky friendly itchy jealous delighted hurt sweet vain
jittery kind furious enthusiastic perturbed loving eager funny zestful
mischievous jumpy keen uncertain dizzy clever miserable naughty yucky
nervous cool guilty nice anxious weak okay patient wacky excited ashamed
proud mixed-up pleased queasy tired questionable ridiculous bashful hopeful
energetic different zonked rambunctious silly quiet overwhelmed
negative sleepy insecure disappointed selfish impatient joyful upset
sensitive vicious beautiful frustrated knowing irritable vibrant worried moody
generous exhilarated youthful active blue obnoxious active
wild sad vulnerable uneasy bored scared curio... ...oubtful
terrific exhausted excited rowdy zealous embarrassed frightened brave giggly

afraid hyperactive wild sad vulnerable uneasy bored scared curious pretty
nasty lonely doubtful terrific exhausted excited rowdy zealous embarrassed
frightened giggly awful weird terrible quarrelsome crazy happy
zany disgusted intimidated greedy lucky friendly itchy jealous delighted hurt
sweet vain jittery kind gross furious enthusiastic perturbed loving eager funny
zestful mischievous jumpy uncertain dizzy clever miserable
yucky nervous cool guilty nice anxious weak okay patient mad wacky excited
ashamed proud mixed-up pleased tired questionable ridiculous bashful
energetic zonked rambunctious silly quiet overwhelmed
negative sleepy glad insecure disappointed timid impatient joyful upset
sensitive vicious beautiful frustrated knowing irritable vibrant worried moody
generous exhilarated youthful active blue obnoxious calm afraid hyperactive
wild sad vulnerable uneasy bored scared pretty nasty lonely doubtful
terrific exhausted excited rowdy zealous embarrassed frightened brave
awful weird terrible quarrelsome crazy stubborn happy zany disgusted
intimidated greedy lucky friendly itchy jealous delighted hurt sweet vain
jittery kind gross furious enthusiastic perturbed loving funny zestful
mischievous jumpy keen uncertain dizzy clever miserable naughty yucky
nervous cool guilty nice anxious weak okay patient mad wacky excited ashamed

LOTS OF Feelings

SHELLEY ROTNER

The Millbrook Press M Brookfield, Connecticut

To my editor, Jean Reynolds,
who always makes me feel valued as an author and photographer.

Copyright © 2003 by Shelley Rotner

Published by
The Millbrook Press, Inc.
2 Old New Milford Road
Brookfield, Connecticut 06804
www.millbrookpress.com

Designed by Michael Nelson

LIBRARY OF CONGRESS CATALOGING-IN-PUBLICATION DATA
Rotner, Shelley.
Lots of feelings / Shelley Rotner.
p. cm.
Summary: Simple text and photographs introduce basic emotions--happy,
grumpy, thoughtful, and more--and how people express them.
ISBN 0-7613-2896-3 (lib. bdg.) -- ISBN 0-7613-2377-5 (trade pbk.)
1. Emotions in children--Juvenile literature. [1. Emotions.] I.
Title.
BF723.E6R68 2003
152.4--dc21
2003006678

Manufactured in Hong Kong
lib. 5 4 3 2 1
pbk. 5 4 3 2 1

We have lots of **feelings.**

Sometimes
we feel
happy,

sometimes
sad.

Sometimes we're **grumpy,**

other
times
excited.

At times we feel shy

8

and
other
times
proud.

We
feel
angry
at
times

and **loving**
other times.

Some
things
surprise
us.

Other things **frighten** us.

13

There are times
we feel
thoughtful

and times
we feel
sleepy.

At different times we feel **serious...**

or **silly...**

17

curious...

18

or **confused.**

Everyone
has
lots of
feelings.

21

How about you?

NOTE FOR PARENTS OR TEACHERS

Lots of Feelings is a book to help children become more aware of their feelings. By learning how to express emotions in appropriate ways, they can better understand themselves and communicate what they are feeling to others. Parents and teachers can use this book to help generate conversation to facilitate this learning process.

Sometimes we don't know exactly how we feel or our faces don't reflect how we really feel inside. Yet how we express ourselves is how we are viewed by others. This is an opportunity for grown-ups to take the time to listen to how children feel and to guide them to appropriate expression so they can be heard and understood. The different faces throughout the book can be used as a means of identifying emotions.

Parents and teachers might use questions such as the following to explore feelings: "What do you think this boy/girl is feeling?" "Have you ever felt this way?" "What would make him feel that way?" "What do you think she would say?" Role playing is another way to help children practice forms of expression. Children can take turns acting out a feeling and their family or friends can respond.

The more we understand our own feelings the more we can understand others. Learning to understand the value of expressing his or her feelings appropriately is an important life skill for a young child and a key element in the development of good communication skills.

Shelley Rotner

afraid hyperactive wild sad vulnerable uneasy bored scared curious pretty
nasty lonely doubtful terrific exhausted excited rowdy zealous embarrassed
frightened giggly awful weird terrible quarrelsome crazy happy
zany disgusted intimidated greedy lucky friendly itchy jealous delighted hurt
sweet vain jittery kind gross furious enthusiastic perturbed loving eager funny
zestful mischievous jumpy uncertain dizzy clever miserable
yucky nervous cool guilty nice anxious weak okay patient mad wacky excited
ashamed proud mixed-up pleased tired questionable ridiculous bashful
energetic zonked rambunctious silly quiet overwhelmed
negative sleepy glad insecure disappointed timid impatient joyful upset
sensitive vicious beautiful frustrated knowing irritable vibrant worried moody
generous exhilarated youthful active blue obnoxious calm afraid hyperactive
wild sad vulnerable uneasy bored scared pretty nasty lonely doubtful
terrific exhausted excited rowdy zealous embarrassed frightened brave
awful weird terrible quarrelsome crazy stubborn happy zany disgusted
intimidated greedy lucky friendly itchy jealous delighted hurt sweet vain
jittery kind gross furious enthusiastic perturbed loving funny zestful
mischievous jumpy keen uncertain dizzy clever miserable naughty yucky
nervous cool guilty nice anxious weak okay patient mad wacky excited ashamed

afraid hyperactive wild sad vulnerable uneasy bored scared curious pretty nasty lonely doubtful terrific exhausted excited rowdy zealous embarrassed frightened giggly awful weird terrible quarrelsome crazy happy zany disgusted intimidated greedy lucky friendly itchy jealous delighted hurt sweet vain jittery kind gross furious enthusiastic perturbed loving eager funny zestful mischievous jumpy uncertain dizzy clever miserable yucky nervous cool guilty nice anxious weak okay patient mad wacky excited ashamed proud mixed-up pleased tired questionable ridiculous bashful energetic zonked rambunctious silly quiet overwhelmed negative sleepy glad insecure disappointed timid impatient joyful upset sensitive vicious beautiful frustrated knowing irritable vibrant worried moody generous exhilarated youthful active blue obnoxious calm afraid hyperactive wild sad vulnerable uneasy bored scared pretty nasty lonely doubtful terrific exhausted excited rowdy zealous embarrassed frightened brave awful weird terrible quarrelsome crazy stubborn happy zany disgusted intimidated greedy lucky friendly itchy jealous delighted hurt sweet vain jittery kind gross furious enthusiastic perturbed loving funny zestful mischievous jumpy keen uncertain dizzy clever miserable naughty yucky nervous cool guilty nice anxious weak okay patient mad wacky excited ashamed